Crochet Secrets

Mia Smith

DEDICATION

To my husband, son and daughter. A million times over I want to say thank you for all of the endless support, encouragement and most importantly love.

CONTENTS

Life for me is better when I crochet!

Mia

"Crochet a row every day to chase the blues away."

Anonymous

SECRETS

Even though I first learned how to crochet from my grandmother many years ago, around the age of eight, with a pink frosted crochet hook and soft white yarn. It wasn't until 2004 when I picked it up again after someone who I never suspected would do any kind of needle craft shared she was crocheting a scarf. It reminded me that I once crocheted and I should try it again. I haven't put it down since.

Over the years I have crocheted pounds of yarn into projects such as Afghans, totes and hand bags, ponchos, hats, scarfs, socks, slippers, baby items and jewelry for gifts, personal use, charity and business ventures. Those countless hours, numerous skeins of yarn, well creased and worn edges of magazines and books, along with many lessons learned and taught have revealed three elements that continued to be present. Those three elements I call Secrets are having Inspiration, practice Relaxation and following Instructions.

You may be wondering why I call them Secrets.

While talking and sharing with others I continued to hear common threads of similar challenges. Finding inspiration, how to relax and understanding instructions. This is in response to those issues. Insight to get at the heart of what it takes to create great crochet projects every-time along with a bit of crochet history.

I am so excited to share with you the secrets I know will make a major difference in your crochet projects. Each one of the secrets are an important ingredient in creating great crochet projects.

YOU ARE A CROCHETER

How did you learn to crochet? Was it your mother who taught you after witnessing her make a poncho? Or your grandmother during a weekend visit where she gifted you a new hook and fun yellow yarn? Possibly you learned by viewing tutorial videos on a crochet site. How you arrived to crochet and what you have done with it is your very special story.

Think back to the early days of deciding which yarn to use, weighing in your hands a plastic or aluminum hook and which project to make. How a deadline may have loomed over your head to get it done in time for the baby's arrival or the Christmas gift. I too think back on those early times where I had sore muscles from gripping the hook and pulling the yarn so tight that I couldn't get the hook in the second row. Not understanding the abbreviations of patterns and gravitated to those written entirely out. Many projects started and getting fed up along the way ripping it out and making knots to finally cutting the yarn throwing the used part in the trash and donating the rest to the thrift store because I couldn't stand to see it. I like you continued on.

Determined to become better at it. Knowing somehow it could be better. Embracing the time and attention it calls for and delving into the creative expression it offers and I learned a skill that was rewarding and something that I could teach others who wanted to learn. Crochet became a part of my life so much so that I was often referred to the Lady who crochets at the school where I taught lessons after school. I pulled it out everywhere I went and welcomed all conversations around it. What I know now about getting inspired, being relaxed while crocheting and following the instructions is something that I wish someone had encouraged me to do early on.

When you crochet there are important things that take place that you may not be aware of. Your mind, body, and emotions are all engaged.

Crochet is a skill and it shows up in very specific ways. Having a skill is the ability to use the knowledge you have learned effectively in order to perform. The knowledge of how to hold a crochet hook, weather your left-handed or right, holding the working yarn and wrapping the yarn round the hook and moving the hook in a particular way to pull the yarn that results in creating loops.

Not only do you perform crochet with your hands your mind is at work also. Your crochet skill enables you to think critically and creativity which is known to use both sides of your brain, the left and the right. Using your left side is when you analyze a pattern or closely examine a crochet item you gain understanding of how it comes together. You can describe it, the amount and size of yarn, size of the crochet hook used and the time it takes to work on it. Being able to problem solve considering all aspects of the project and to discover a solution is from both sides of the brain. Creativity is the right side of the brain and appears through imagining. Imagining involves thinking through the final project you want to make and the possible methods to apply to reach a desired outcome. Simply put your right and left sides of your brain are at work when you crochet.

Can you believe crochet has its own language? It does. The name of the stitches; chain, slip stich, single crochet, double crochet or half double for example and of the 30 plus actions are written as abbreviations in patterns.

It looks like; ch, sl st, sc, dc and hdc. Lots of practice and intention are needed to be able to read a crochet pattern and understand it. The truth is that you have learned another language.

You are a Crocheter. A skilled, creative, and resourceful needle artist. Be encouraged in this truth knowing it matters and while creating it brings in more inspiration, lots of relaxation and building your understanding as you apply following instructions.

A Time of Reflection

Who was that special person that taught you to crochet? Is that someone you still share crochet with?

____

____

____

____

____

____

____

____

____

____

____

____

____

____

____

What is your favorite memory of that time?

____

____

____

____

____

____

____

____

____

____

____

____

____

____

In what ways did that experience positively impact your life?

CROCHET MATTERS

Crochet matters and what we get from it matters too. We know the word is French and it has a bit of controversy as to its origins and depending on what historian you talk with one may say it was in Europe where the first needle art magazine mentioned crochet. Another person may say it was the fine delicate looped fabric found in ancient archeological finds near Egypt. Someone else may even say forget the others and lets only focus on the modern-day evidence of what we know crochet to be today. Whichever one you ascribe to we know it enables us to express and get the tangible benefits and rewards that come from the needle art.

To create it a hooked instrument was used to grab thread to make a delicate looped fabric. Early as 1824 printed patterns were available in European countries to make the popular delicate crochet lace. However, a large majority learned the skills and patterns by passing them down from mother to daughter, friend to friend and neighbor to neighbor.

The years into the 20th century as manufacturing

methods improved. Offering developments and improvements of yarns and hooks coupled with easier to follow written and illustrated patterns that were in popular magazines, helped to provide more access. It was the yarn machine called the Spinning Jenny invented in 1786 by Richard Arkwright powered by water and spun more and stronger threads for yarn making, needless to say made yarn more widely available.

What we do know crochet projects require twice as much yarn than its sister needle art knitting. Those who create with it say it is easy to understand. It works up fast, much faster than other needle arts and it is effortless to add onto or change directions with a pattern or free styling, which is really popular. Rewarding is the word I would and have used when describing crochet to someone. We want a needle craft we can get satisfaction and accomplishment from. Most people are not seeking a never-ending project.

With the innovation of mass-produced yarn, crochet hooks and more widely available publications featuring the needle art. These options sprung open wide the access to anyone who would want to learn the skill.

The 1960's and 1970's saw an explosion of crochet items such as ponchos, shorts, vests and the ever-popular granny square. The granny square could be found every-where such as fashion run ways, magazines and television. Personally, I appreciate the wide spread embrace. I do need to be honest, for many years the picture that came to many of our minds when thinking of crochet was … a grandmother making a blanket. Often referred to as something your grandmother does. Despite the fashionable images in magazines and runways. I am so glad to say that that image has grown and although grandmothers do crochet there is also the college student in her dorm lounge crocheting, the working woman on her lunch break getting a few rows in or the guy who crochets while enjoying a cup of coffee in a local shop. All types of people crochet and it is a beautiful thing to see.

Hooks are made of aluminum, plastic, steel, wood, and combinations of two materials. Online, big box stores, local yarn stores or even your neighborhood thrift store offer crochet hooks. The hook is the tool, as is the hammer for the carpenter, the curling iron to the hair stylist and the hand mixer to the baker. In other words, you need it to create great crochet projects. However, matching your needs to the right crochet hook can more often than not be a challenge.

What I discovered after making several projects and using all types of hooks was one that is comfortable in my hands. That hook allows the yarn to glide and even makes it more relaxing in my hands instead of creating muscle tension from the repetitive movement of working on stiches. Those crafters who have years of experience can attest to the importance of the right, well made, perfect fit and light weight hook that can uplift the crochet creation time. Something beginners are not yet aware of.

Finding the hook or hooks that work best for you gives further enjoyment of creating with crochet. I will have to strongly suggest if it is in your budget to buy two of your favorites just in case you lose sight of one that has fallen into the deep dark spaces in between the couch cushions.

Crochet does matter and has a long rich history and we get to experience all of the wonderful innovations today.

☐

A Time of Reflection

What were the yarns, magazines/books and hooks you used during the beginning of your crochet life?

____

____

____

____

____

____

____

____

____

____

____

____

____

Are there tools and yarns today that were not available when you first crocheted?

If you could imagine the future of crochet 10 years from now, what do you wish to see?

INSPIRATION

What initially motivates me when I think of creating a great crochet project is Inspiration. Being inspired which is a feeling of excitement, encouragement and the experience of breathing life into something, will motivate you towards envisioning the project and it also creates a connection to the piece. Many more times than not, our crochet projects begin with a request from someone else. They admire a scarf or hat you have crocheted and exclaim how they want one, two or even three and of course in their favorite colors.

For others you may be a part of a needle craft group and one of the activities is to create crochet pieces to give to charity. The charities may include items for a women's shelter, crochet squares to assemble for blankets for the American Red Cross, or hats for infants in a hospital. Those reasons for creating those crochet items are good and they meet a desire to give to others who are in a place where help is needed, all of which is beneficial and rewarding.

However, you should zero in on those things that personally inspire you. What are they? It may be a colorful and fragrant flower, the sight and sounds of cool and refreshing ocean waves, a delicious and beautifully decorated chocolate cupcake, a new pair of red high heeled pumps or an elaborately painted multi colored tea cup. There are other sources of inspiration to breathe life into a crochet project such as flipping through the pages of a magazine or book showing trendy sweaters, home décor or cute baby items. I have only mentioned a few things that may be considered a source of inspiration. What does inspire you will be special and unique to you.

Your reaction to being inspired to crochet, is specifically that an action. It shows up when you are selecting which yarn(s), hook and pattern or the creation of a self-design and it fosters a connection that makes a positive impact. Going to the yarn store to touch with your fingers the softness or thickness of the yarns you are considering. Seeing the brightness or warmth of the array of endless color options and although you probably don't need another one, viewing the many options of crochet hooks and notions.

My first truly inspired crochet piece was about 10

years ago when my daughter shared that she loved purple and wanted a blanket in purple. That was my inspiration to crochet a twin sized granny square patterned afghan featuring three shades of purple with light yellow and white accents. That afghan is her favorite and mine too. I am connected to it, having had many bedtime stories with her reading and snuggling under it and watching movies on Saturday nights comfortable on the couch.

I have found, along with the testimony of others being inspired and excited to crochet enables the completion of the project. Those times when I have started and wasn't inspired, more often than not it was left unfinished and tossed in a bag stuffed in a closet or in a storage bin. Something I'm sure we all can relate to. Once you have experienced the inspiration and connection to a crochet piece, it should be the high bar you reach for when deciding and know it is an important part of creating a great crochet project.

The things shared are yours to adapt and adjust to your preference to be inspired knowing it will be a great addition to your crochet involvement. The next secret to creating great crochet is Relaxation and it is a wonderful compliment to Inspiration

A Time of Reflection

What was your most fulfilling crochet project to make?

____

____

____

____

____

____

____

____

____

____

____

____

____

Do you share your crochet inspiration with others? If no why not?

____

____

____

____

____

____

____

____

____

____

____

____

What are the people, places or things that inspire you to crochet?

____

____

____

____

____

____

____

____

____

____

____

____

____

____

RELAXATION

Teaching crochet classes at a local library, recreation center or community school I have continually found new and experienced Crocheters tend to hunch their shoulders and clamp their teeth together. The frustration and tension are evident. The upside is they are engaging in crochet which they want to however, the time spent while doing it is making tension in their body and thoughts. Immediately, I encourage them to relax their shoulders, to smile and tell them they can do it. That usually makes the difference. In that moment it becomes more enjoyable. When there is a new pattern or stitch, I'm learning I too remind myself to relax my shoulders and unclench my teeth, funny after all these years.

Hearing the word Relaxation should evoke calmness and peace. When settling in that special spot on the couch or chair and pulling out the yarn, hook and pattern of the project to be created, when embracing the time thoughts about problems or concerns should fade away and the focus becomes the needle art. Being totally in the state of happiness, bliss or feeling that source of delight.

You may be wondering how it actually happens. Relaxation happens through the repetitive movement of the act of crocheting. Focusing on yarning over, inserting the hook, pulling up loop(s) and repeating. Each stich is an accomplishment, each row is an achievement, and the growth of the fabric shows. Try to enjoy what has and is happening in the moment. Intentionally take deep breaths and relax your shoulders and make sure you're sitting position is comfortable and supported and embrace the great benefit of relaxation that comes from crocheting. An online article in the New York Times written by Jane Brody, January 25, 2016 states, "Dr. Herbert Benson, a pioneer in mind/body medicine says that the repetitive action of needlework can induce a relaxed state like that is associated with mediation and yoga". The opposite of not relaxing when crocheting is being unfocused, missed stiches, not productive and frustration. Relaxation is a go-to experience I yearn for when crocheting and it has to be present. It will enable us to create great crochet projects.

This second secret to creating great crochet is yours to put into practice in a way that best suits you. However, the next secret is one many push-back on. This era of on-line video instruction and crafters posting their versions of the needle art can pose a challenge to promoting the art in a way that genuinely shows the stiches and methods. On the back page you will find reputable websites offering clear, consistent and helpful instructions as to how to create the scores of crochet stiches done as the industry standard. There are tremendous opportunities when you follow instructions resulting in experiencing my third secret to creating great crochet projects.

A Time of Reflection

Do you find it difficult or easy to relax? What have been the challenges? When done try one of the tips in this chapter.

How does relaxation show up when you crochet?

Are there specific benefits from relaxing while crocheting that you have felt?

____

____

____

____

____

____

____

____

____

____

____

____

____

INSTRUCTION

Being an experienced or newcomer to crochet, either level, it is my assumption that you know or are learning the Instructions of crochet. The instructions of the needle art are the foundation for you to follow along as you crochet stitches and finish projects. Instructions enable you to produce a piece that has lasting quality. The importance of following instructions was taught to you as a young student and how to follow directions were all in the effort for you to know how to perform a particular skill. As an adult those same skills and abilities are applied the same today as you progress and learn crochet.

What does it look like? It enables you to get to know the detailed ways a pattern is created and when you have practiced those specifics it then becomes an addition to your skill set. If gauge is a part of the pattern often times this is skipped however, I urge you to take the time to do the gauge swatch.

Gauge is simply crocheting a 4inch x 4inch square using the recommended yarn, hook and stich. You will measure the piece and count how many stiches there are within an inch. The pattern will provide additional information. Doing so will enable you to more confidently tackle the pattern and know of any adjustments you may need to make with your tension or hook. This will save time, yarn and avoid frustration. It also builds your skills as you practice new patterns and stiches. When creating gauge swatches, you apply that knowledge to future projects. If you are someone who creates their own crochet designs without a pre-written pattern, I encourage you to also create a swatch of what you have in mind and work out any kinks that may come up.

Finishing, more often described as weaving in ends, is another aspect of following instructions that when done as recommended makes the appearance of your item more pleasurable to the eye. The other rewards to following instructions is the satisfaction of completing a piece that expresses your creativity and making something useful.

Each art form has its foundations and crochet is no different. There are some who say they just make up the stiches and call it crochet. Crochet has its own look and feel just as knitting and weaving and producing items following the DNA (i.e., pattern or design) of crochet also benefit you in that your piece will also be of quality. The specific and detailed ways to create a chain, single, double and treble crochet stiches and from there are endless possibilities to create other stitches to make patterns. You can also find affordable encyclopedias of crochet stiches and motifs providing clear instructions of dozens of examples.

On the resource page you will see websites for you to visit to get clear and helpful instructions. With any skill, as you practice and experience inspiration and relaxation you become better at it and you will be able to see your growth in the outcome of the items you make which is tremendously fulfilling.

A Time of Reflection

Have you found it difficult in your life to follow instructions? What does that look like when it happens?

Are there things you did, or help received in order to overcome that challenge?

____

____

____

____

____

____

____

____

____

____

____

____

How would you encourage someone else to follow instructions?

THE CROCHET LIFE

Over 190 years is the amount of time crochet the needle art has been done by women and some men all over the world. Becoming more familiar with the history of crochet and how it has developed gives us a deeper appreciation. Seeing crochet is an important part of our lives it would make sense that when we crochet for it to be an all-around good experience.

I urge you to embrace your inspiration. What is an inspiration to you may not be for me and that is okay. The point is that you are inspired and it fuels your crochet project. A question to ask another crocheter is, "what inspires you to crochet?" Sharing with each other the reasons why I hope will spread goodness.

All of us are not in the same stage in life. You may be a college student, work 60 hours a week at a corporate job, mother of four school age children or a man who designs websites. Wherever you are in life when you stop to crochet that time should be relaxing. The concerns of the day and frustrations of the future should fade away and the rhythm of the hook, movement of the yarn, un-hunching your shoulders and maybe an extra pillow tucked closely by your side can bring relaxation. Have you experience relaxation while crocheting? If so, consider sharing this secret with others.

Having a skill that is beneficial to yourself and others is a great opportunity. More importantly you get to create for yourself and for others beautiful and useful pieces that have lasting quality. Following pattern instructions or writing one yourself to create a crochet piece is a skill you will have for the rest of your life. Consider there are young people you know, friends or family members who would also like to learn this skill. You could provide them the instructions and emphasize the importance of following them so they will be able to produce great crochet projects.

Crochet has enriched my life in many ways. It has brought me great friendships, fed my need to constantly learn by the skills of learning new patterns and stiches, keeps my critical and analyzing skills sharp, enables me to express my creativity and give gifts of beauty and usefulness. I wish for you endless hours of crochet creativity where Inspiration, Relaxation and following Instructions are a doable and good thing in your life.□

A Time of Reflection

In what ways has crochet enriched your life?

ABOUT THE AUTHOR

Mia Smith is an accomplished needle artist specializing in Crochet and Sewing. Taught both around the age of eight by her grandmother she blossomed as a sewer in her teen years, continuing to this day and picked up a crochet hook again later as an adult.

As an author she shares the great things about needle arts and especially enjoys promoting the African American story in it. She has been invited to teach and present at libraries, community groups, schools and businesses and has over twelve years of providing instruction to new and experienced learners through classes and one-on-one lessons.

Her first publication Crochet Secret is soon to be followed by other crochet pattern books titled Crochet Culture, Kente Crochet and Crochet Kuumba. She has a B. A. and has continued her learning by obtaining a Diploma in Seamstress and Dressmaking an active member of the Crochet Guild of America and a Certified Crochet Instructor from the Craft Yarn Council.

Dear Reader,

You are invited to visit www.untangleyarnacademy.com to learn about the crochet classes I offer for children, teens, and adults also you will see available other publications at www.amazon.com/author/miasmith

Yours in Yarn,

Mia

DEFINITIONS

Abbreviations- the method that writers of crochet instructions use

American Red Cross – a United States humanitarian organization that provides emergency assistance and disaster relief

Crochet – consists of interlocking of looped stitches formed with a single thread or yarn and a hooked needle

Crocheter – a person who creates crochet

Needle Art – the use of an instrument hooked or strait to move thread or yarn to make a stand-alone fabric or a backing or netting or paper

Weaving – is a method of two yarns or threads that are crossed at right angles to create fabric

RESOURCES

Crochet www.crochet.org

UnTangle Yarn Academy www.untangleyarnacademy.com

Crochet www.redheart.com

Knitting and Crochet www.craftyarncouncil.com

Made in the USA
Monee, IL
07 July 2026

56551654R00031